A Youngster's Guidebook
of How to Play
BASEBALL

Skills, drills
Tips & Tricks

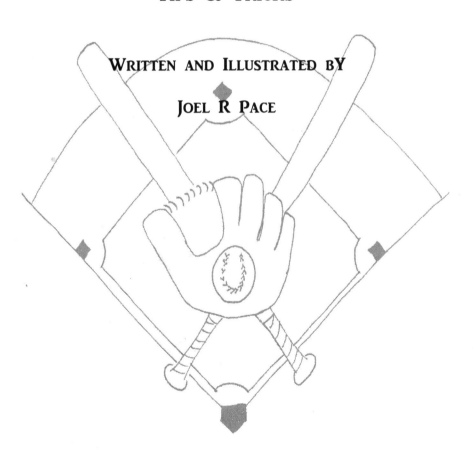

Written and Illustrated by

Joel R Pace

This Book is Property of...

My name is: _____

My nickname is: _____

My favorite baseball team is:

_____

My favorite baseball player is:

_____

My favorite position is:

_____

My favorite thing about Baseball is:

_____

_____

_____

_____

Hey Kids: You'll Hear These From Coach A LOT!

WHERE'S THE PLAY?

Hustle!

HAVE FUN

BE A HERO

It's a game of inches and seconds

CHARACTER

Be a Good Sport

Keep your Eye on the Ball

100% Commitment

Cut the Ball in Half

STRIVE FOR EXCELLENCE

Glory is Forever

100% EFFORT

CLUTCH HITTER!

Catch the Ball With 2 Hands

Be Alert & Ready

PAIN IS ONLY AN INSTANT

Stay down on the ball

A YOUNGSTER'S GUIDEBOOK
OF HOW TO PLAY
BASEBALL
SKILLS, DRILLS
TIPS & TRICKS

CONTENTS:

FOR YOUNG BASEBALL PLAYERS THAT DARE TO BE GREAT...

 YOU ARE PLAYING THE BEST GAME ON EARTH!!

 YOU MUST PLEASE THE BASEBALL GODS
BY GIVING YOUR BEST EFFORT!

 YOU WILL CRUSH THE BALL, MAKE DIVING CATCHES,
AND GET DIRTY.

 BASEBALL WILL BUILD YOU UP,
MAKE YOU TOUGH N STRONG,
GIVE YOU STORIES OF GLORY AND
MEMORIES FOR A LIFETIME.

 PLAYING BASEBALL IS A BETTER PASTTIME
THAN PLAYING VIDEO GAMES,
WATCHING MOVIES, OR
WATCHING TV-GET OUT AND PLAY!

 BASEBALL MAY GIVE YOU BUMPS N BRUISES, AND
ACHES 'N PAINS, BUT YOU'LL BE HUNGRY FOR MORE!!

 PAIN IS ONLY AN INSTANT, BUT GLORY IS FOREVER.
SO, GET IN FRONT OF THE BALL AND MAKE THE PLAY!

 HEROES ARE REMEMBERED AND LEGENDS NEVER DIE!!

 TRY YOUR HARDEST AND STRIVE TO BE EXCELLENT

Hey KidS: WELCOME To THE BaSeBaLL CLUB!

I'm COACH: I'm here to help you understand and play the game of BASEBALL...

Really, it's easy. There are **10 SIMPLE LESSONS** to help improve your game immediately!

Firstly: **BaSEBaLL** is one of the greatest games on Earth.

There's something about the **-CRaCK-** of the BAT,

the **ROAR** of the crowd,

the **WHItE LInES**,

and **SMELL** of **FRESH CUT GRASS**

that makes us crave

BUBBLE GUM, SUNFLOWER SEEDS

and to GET DIRTY!

Secondly: **BaSEBaLL** is a lot like **LIFE**:

The more **EFFORt** you give,

the more **HUStLE** and **COURaGE** you have,

and the deeper you

UnDERStanD THE GAME,

you will be able to

MaKE tHE PLaY and

win as a **TEaM**....

PAY Attention!

...ALL OUT BABY!!!

HoW to USe tHiS HandbooK:

Kids, this handbook is for you to COLOR IN and TAKE NOTES.

MEMORIZE THE FORMULAS!

Practice the A-B-C step-by-step process,
REPEAT them.
Take a breath and DO IT AGAIN!!!
After a **1000** times, you'll develop muscle memory
and your mechanics will become automatic!

Color in all the illustrations. Follow the cues in the visualization
exercises. 80% of Baseball is mental. Visualize success!

Have you heard 'Practice makes perfect?"

I'd like to make one correction to that:

PERFECT PRACTICE MAKES PERFECT

PREPARATION is the key. Be prepared!

EQUIPMENT LIST:
√GLOVE, √HAT, √CLEATS, √WATER, √SNACK

LASTLY: **RESPECT** & **Honor** the game!

BE A **GOOD SPORT**! COMPETE HARD & IMPROVE!

DON'T LET THE SCOREBOARD DETERMINE YOUR SUCCESS!

& **BE a WINNER**, even in DEFEAT! That means:

DON'T THROW YOUR HAT OR GLOVE OR KICK DIRT in disgust!

HAVE FUN, WORK HARD & **PLAY BALL!**

...IT'S GAMETIME!!!!

IS the rUNNer

SaFe or oUt?

Color in the illustration and remember:
The umpire will LISTEN to hear what happens first:
Does the ball hit the glove or does the foot hit the bag?
If you're the runner, DON'T LOOK AT THE BALL and
RUN HARD.

LESSON 1

tHE Basics OF Baseball

"Baseball is a 'A GAME OF INCHES AND SECONDS.'
There are a lot of situations in baseball.
You must know the play before the hit, and react quickly to
the ball so you can get the out.
If you are up to bat, you might hit a deep 'sacrifice fly' because
you have a man on 3rd base and they can tag up and score!
By KNOWING THE GAME, you can create a better strategy to win!

REMEMBER: OutsMarting your Opponent is tHE naME OF tHE GaME...

The Objectives for this Lesson are to learn:

> The BASICS of BASEBALL : OFFENSE and DEFENSE :
> KEY TERMS : BIG IDEAS

THE BASICS OF BASEBALL
iN a NutSHeLL:

In baseball, there are **9** positions on the field.

#1 Pitcher,	#4 Second Base,	#7 Left Field,
#2: Catcher,	#5 Third Base,	#8 Center Field,
#3 1st Base,	#6 Shortstop,	#9 Right Field

The **PitcHER** throws the ball to the **CatCHER**.

The **BattER** attempts to hit the ball and GET ON BASE to become a **RunnER**.

The **RunnERS** try to cross HOME PLATE to **SCORE**.

ON defense:

The **INFIELDERS** and **OUtFIELDERS** try to **MaKE a PLaY** when the ball is hit to them to GET THE RUNNERS **OUT!....**

EACH team gets **3** OUTS in an **inning** ... The team with the most **RUNS** at the end of the game **WIns**!

There is **MUCH** MORE to it, but the more you know about **FORCE** OUTS, how to execute **DOUBLE PLAYS**, CRUSH **LInED−DRIVES**, lay **SaCRIFICE BUnts** and WHAT TO DO when the ball is **Hit** to **YOU**, with skills to **FIELD a GROUND BALL**, and **CatCH** a **FLY BALL**, and **THROW ACCURATELY** to your target the more **CHANCE** you will have to **WIN**!

Common **BASEBALL TERMS**

BASEBALL DIAMOND   FAIR BALL   FOUL BALL   FORCE OUT

STRIKE   BALL   OUTS   INNINGS   SINGLE   DOUBLE   TRIPLE

PICKLE   TAGGING UP   SPORTSMANSHIP   HOME RUN

BATTER UP!
Read the chapter and come back to answer
these questions:

1. What does the PITCHER and
     BATTER do:

Pitcher:

_____

_____

Batter: _____

_____

2. What is the rule for a FOUL BALL:

_____

_____

_____

_____

3. Explain a FORCE OUT?

_____
_____
_____
_____
_____

4. Describe a DOUBLE PLAY?

_____
_____
_____
_____
_____

5. What is a TRIPLE?

_____
_____
_____
_____
_____

6. Give an example of
     GOOD SPORTSMANSHIP:

_____
_____
_____
_____
_____

BASEBALL BASICS

BASEBALL TERMS
DEFINED

The BASICS of BASEBALL

BASEBALL DIAMOND: Common name of the field that baseball is played on. From 500 feet up, it looks like a diamond

FAIR BALL: A 'playable' ball hit between 1st baseline and 3rd baseline.

FOUL BALL: A ball hit outside the 1st or 3rd base line. If ball is hit In the air, it is 'playable' by the defense for an OUT. If it is hit on the ground, it is not 'playable' for an out, but may count as a STRIKE. If the batter has 2 strikes and hits a non-playable foul ball, they are 'STILL ALIVE' and continue to bat. The STRIKE does not count.
PAY ATTENTION: If the ball rolls in foul territory before 1st or 3rd base, then jumps fair, it will be FAIR.
STRATEGY: Kick the ball MORE foul!

FORCE OUT: When runner's occupy each base up to the lead base, for example: runner on 2nd, AND 1st, there is a force out at 3rd. If a runner is on 1st base, there is a FORCE OUT at 2nd. There is ALWAYS a FORCE OUT at 1st base. If a runner is on 2nd, but 1st base is unoccupied, then there is not a FORCE OUT at 3rd, only at 1st base. The DEFENSE does NOT need to Tag the runner. Tagging the base executes the OUT.

STRIKE: A pitch in the strike zone (the zone directly above HOME PLATE between the knees and chest of the batter). A FOUL BALL also counts as a STRIKE. A batter gets 3 STRIKES before they are OUT.

BALL: An unhittable pitch outside the STRIKE ZONE. A BATTER gets 4 BALLS for a 'WALK' to 1st BASE!

OUT: When the DEFENSE puts out a runner or batter either on the base path or at the plate in any number of ways. The OFFENSE gets 3 OUTS before changing sides to DEFENSE.

INNINGS: 3 outs for each team (6 outs total) make up 1 INNING

PICKLE: The baserunner might get caught by the DEFENSE trying to get an extra base and is caught in a 'run down.'
IF YOU ARE ON DEFENSE: Whatever you do, DON'T give up the next bag

TAGGING UP: When a baserunner attempts to advance to the next base AFTER a fly ball is CAUGHT by the DEFENSE.

THE OBJECT OF THE GAME

OFFENSE:

The team that is UP TO BAT is the offense and they try to get as many RUNS across HOME PLATE as possible. The offense gets on BASE by **WALKING**, OR hitting **SINGLES, DOUBLES, TRIPLES, HOME RUNS** or **GRAND SLAMS.**

A WALK is when the PITCHER throws 4 BALLS. The BATTER earns a WALK to 1st BASE.

A SINGLE is when the ball is hit and the runner is SAFE at FIRST BASE.

A DOUBLE is when the ball is hit and the runner is SAFE at SECOND BASE.

A TRIPLE is when the ball is hit and the runner is SAFE at THIRD BASE.

A HOME RUN is when the ball is hit and the runner rounds all the bases and is SAFE at HOME PLATE.

A GRAND SLAM is when a player hits a HOME RUN with BASES LOADED (with runners on all bases)!

DEFENSE: The DEFENSE in the field tries to get the offense OUT and limit their runs.

Ways to get OUTS: **FIELDING GROUNDERS, CATCHING FLY BALLS, FORCE OUTS, DOUBLE PLAYS,** and **STRIKE OUTS...**

There are LOTS of ways to get them OUT!

If you make a mistake...**SHAKE IT OFF!** get READY for the next pitch!

REMEMBER YOU NEED 3 OUTS!!!

DEFENSIVE POSITIONS

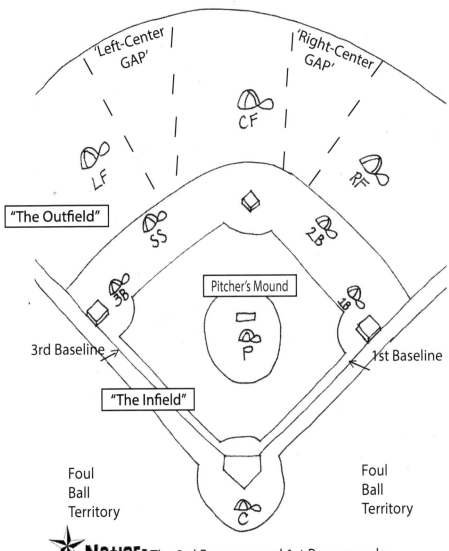

NOTICE: The 3rd Baseman and 1st Baseman play evenly with the bag.
The Shortstop and 2nd Baseman play DEEPER toward the back of the infield.
This allows **SS** and **2B** to 'BACKUP' 3B and 1B...

Position by Number
#1 Pitcher (P)
#2 Catcher (C)
#3 1st Baseman (1B)
#4 2nd Baseman (2B)
#5 3rd Baseman (3B)
#6 Shortstop (SS)
#7 Left Fielder (LF)
#8 Center Fielder (CF)
#9 Right Fielder (RF)

6-4-3 DOUBLE PLAY

When sports broadcasters say: "that was an incredible 6-4-3 Double Play," what that REALLY means is: the Shortstop (#6) threw the ball to the 2nd Baseman (#4), who tagged second base and threw the ball to the 1st Baseman (#3), who tagged 1st base for the out.

CHaiN oF CoMMaNd:

THE **CatCHER** is the GENERAL of your DEFENSE on the field.

He oversees the whole picture of the field.
He calls out the play to everybody, like if someone is threatening to STEAL A BASE he'll yell "WATCH THE RUNNER!!"

THE **SHORtStOP** is the CAPTAIN of the INFIELD.

He'll announce how many outs there are and where the next play will be.

THE **CEntER FiELDER** is the LEADER of the OUTFIELD.

The outfield is considered the center fielder's territory. If a ball is hit between the center fielder and the left or right fielder, and they are both running for it, then the left or right fielder allow the center fielder get the ball.

⭐ What other **BACKUP** assignments exist? ⭐
How about RF backing up 1B? Or, LF backing up 3B....

HOW THE GAME IS CALLED

1 Ball
2 Strikes
1 Out

UMPIRES call the BALLS, STRIKES, OUTS.

3 ways you get A **STRIKE**

1) when the ball goes through the STRIKE ZONE

2) when a batter SWINGS at a pitch and misses it, or

3) FOULS it off...a FOUL with 2 strikes is NOT a strike out... YOU ARE NOT OUT! You are **STAYING ALIVE**!

STRIKE!

Don't Get FRAZZLED... you get 3 strikes!

KAPOW!

be patient... find your pitch... and cut the ball in half!

GOOD SPORT BAD SPORT

BASEBALL IS aBOUt HOW YOU aPPROACH tHE GaME

Are you READY TO HUSTLE? Are you FOCUSED on the PLAY?
Did you practice PERFECTLY so you play PERFECTLY?
Because that other team showed up--
Are you READY to play your A GAME?

GOOD SPORTSMANSHIP is about HAVING FUN,
APPLAUDING good plays for EVERYONE--even your
OPPONENT--and TRYING your BEST!

Baseball is a TEAM SPORT that requires 9 PLAYERS to
SUPPORT & ENCOURAGE each other, BUILD CONFIDENCE
in each other and PLAY TOGETHER to COMPETE and IMPROVE!

WINNERS Even in DEFEAT:

Even if your team comes up on the LOSING END of
the game, CONGRATULATE the other team--they
PLAYED HARD! And, KEEP YOUR CHIN UP! You played
hard, too!

BE A WINNER!!!

2 Ways YOU can BE a GOOD SPORT:

1) If one of your teammates made an error, how can you help lift
their spirits? _____
_____
_____

2) If a teammate gets mad for striking out, how can you make
them feel better? _____
_____
_____

Baseball Basics Word Search

```
I  R  N  W  E  W  C  F  N  E  U  Y  A  A  G
L  S  U  P  J  M  C  W  A  A  L  E  S  G  U
I  T  R  I  P  Y  S  R  D  I  L  P  N  B  L
F  U  E  H  S  O  I  T  W  B  R  I  I  G  G
E  O  M  S  Y  I  T  F  U  L  G  I  N  R  H
K  R  O  N  T  T  N  O  B  G  Z  B  N  O  T
I  Q  H  A  A  D  D  G  A  M  A  B  I  P  W
R  F  H  M  H  A  N  T  L  S  N  R  N  Y  L
T  A  Z  S  Y  O  O  E  E  K  P  G  P  U
S  L  B  T  Y  N  E  B  M  Q  D  U  S  F  G
Y  L  T  R  Q  H  A  R  D  A  M  L  O  E  K
H  A  M  O  F  L  X  R  M  B  I  U  R  C  E
G  B  C  P  L  N  X  X  W  P  L  D  E  R  J
V  Y  G  S  U  Q  T  Y  D  U  I  M  X  O  B
O  U  P  T  G  E  L  K  C  I  P  V  E  F  W
```

FIND and CIRCLE the following words in the Word Search:

Ball	Innings	Baseball	Out
Diamond	Pickle	Double	Single
Fair	Sportsmanship	Force	Strike
Foul	Tagging	Home Run	Triple

DO yOU LiKe to WatcH BaseBaLL oN TV?_____

Did you LearN anytHiNg NeW iN tHis LessoN? LiSt anytHing yOu
LearNed:_____

_____

GREAT INNING!

Finish the inning by answering these questions...

1. Explain where the SS and 2B lineup to play:

_____

_____

_____

_____

_____

2. How many OUTS in an INNING?

_____

_____

_____

_____

3. What is a STRIKE ZONE?

_____

_____

_____

_____

_____

4. What does TAGGING UP mean?

_____

_____

_____

_____

5. What is a PICKLE?

_____

_____

_____

_____

6. What is a GRAND SLAM?

_____

_____

_____

_____

The BASICS of BASEBALL

OK, Team–
Where's
the Play?

COLOR IN COACH. REMEMBER TO LISTEN AND PAY ATTENTION.
HE'S HERE TO HELP.

Lesson 2

Where to Make the Play

"Before the next pitch, look around at the bases and observe the situation. Is there a force out? Is there a baserunner that can steal? At each and every pitch, you should yell to your teammates two things:
    1) The number of outs
            &
    2) Where to make the next play"

The Objectives for this Lesson are to learn:

> DEFENSIVE TERRITORY : COVERAGE :
> SITUATIONS : CUTOFFS 2, 3, 4

WHERE'S THE PLAY?

Have you ever been in the field and really didn't know what to do if the ball came your way?

And then *CRACK* the ball came right at you?

Oh NO!   **WHAT NOW???**

CAREFUL: it'll burn your hand like a HOT POTATO!

GET RID OF IT! ...But where to???

You have to know where to make the play

BEFORE tHE BaLL IS HIt tO YOU!!

Different situations will exist on the field ALL THE TIME, so you will have to know what to do with the ball IMMEDIATELY. Figure it out before the pitch...

Fortunately, you have two options:

1) Listen for the play from the Shortstop

2) Ask the Coach.

Common BASEBALL TERMS

BACKING UP   DOUBLE PLAY   CALLING A BALL

FREEZING A RUNNER   RANGE   CUT OFF MAN   ERROR

BATTER UP! Read the chapter and come back to answer these questions:

Test YOUR Skills! Get a GOOD HIT!

1. What does it mean to BACK UP your teammate? _____

_____

2. What's a 'CUT OFF MAN'?: _____

_____

3. What's the RANGE of the 3rd baseman? _____

_____

4. Describe yourself CALLING A BALL? What does that sound like?

_____

5. What is a common DOUBLE PLAY you might know about'? _____

_____

BASEBALL TERMS DEFINED

BACKING UP: When a player tries to get the ball AFTER their teammate attempted, but failed, to get the ball. They are said to have 'backed up' the player.
Example: the Shortstop backs up the 3rd baseman.

DOUBLE PLAY (DP): 2 outs are recorded on the SAME play.

> Common DPs are 6-4-3, 4-6-3, 1-6-3. An uncommon double play is the 5-2-3, and works only if bases are loaded.
> The 5-4-3 is called "AROUND THE HORN."

CALLING A BALL: When the ball is hit in the air--DOESN'T MATTER if the ball is hit on the INFIELD or OUTFIELD--you must "CALL THE BALL" by yelling "I got it, I got it!" over and over. Get under it and CATCH it!

ERROR: A playable ball that was misplayed. Results in a RUNNER that SHOULD HAVE BEEN OUT!

FREEZING A RUNNER: You FREEZE a runner when they are not forced to run on a hit ball and the infielder, if played well, will take a moment and 'look the runner back' before making their play to the 1st baseman.

RANGE: The COVERAGE a player has on the field. How far they can DEFEND against HITS or FOUL BALLS and MAKE THE OUT!

CUT OFF MAN: The player that supports his teammate by 'cutting off' the throw--usually from deep in the OUTFIELD--to a target on the INFIELD.

Where to make the play

DEFENSIVE TERRITORY...

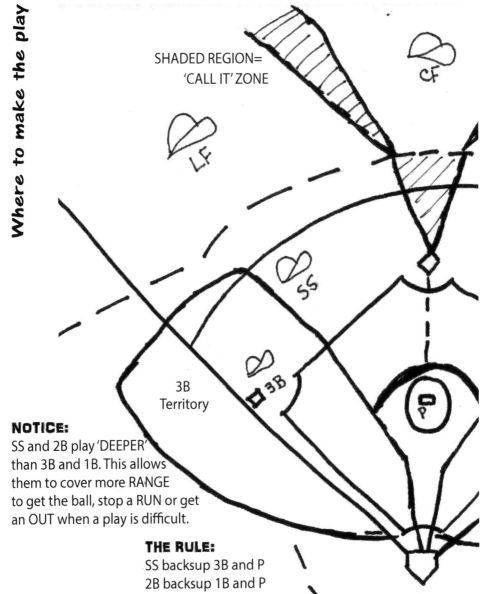

SHADED REGION=
'CALL IT' ZONE

CF

LF

SS

3B
Territory

3B

P

NOTICE:
SS and 2B play 'DEEPER'
than 3B and 1B. This allows
them to cover more RANGE
to get the ball, stop a RUN or get
an OUT when a play is difficult.

THE RULE:
SS backsup 3B and P
2B backsup 1B and P

C

ALWAYS CALL THE BALL!!...

...& COVERAGE

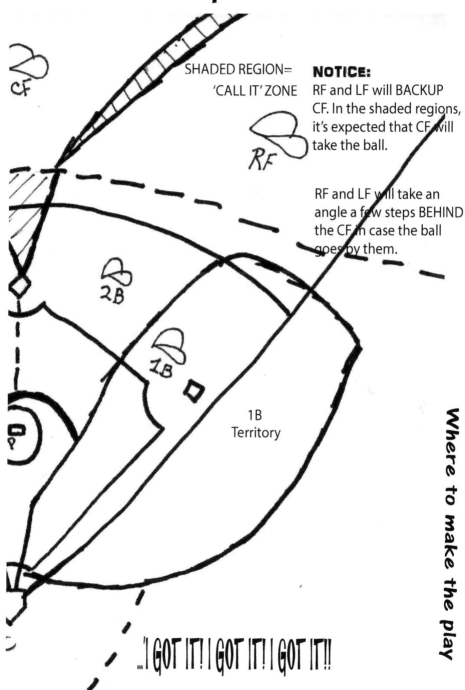

SHADED REGION= 'CALL IT' ZONE

CF

RF

2B

1B

1B Territory

P

NOTICE:
RF and LF will BACKUP CF. In the shaded regions, it's expected that CF will take the ball.

RF and LF will take an angle a few steps BEHIND the CF in case the ball goes by them.

...I GOT IT! I GOT IT! I GOT IT!!

Where to make the play

What to do When...

★ CUT 2, CUT 2 ★

If there is an imaginary line running through the middle of the field.

If the ball is hit to LEFT or CF FIELD, the SS becomes a CUTOFF for the 2nd Baseman who covers 2nd Base....

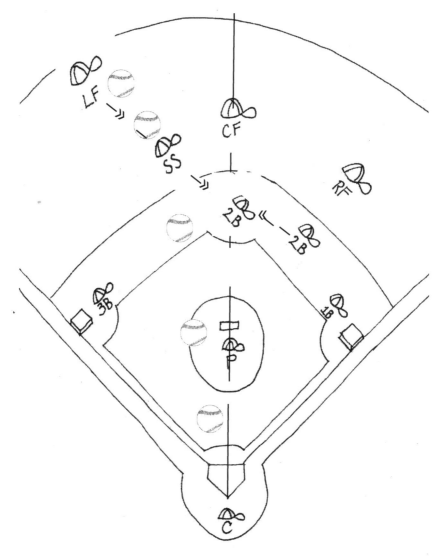

...a Ball is Hit to the OutField

★ CUT 3, CUT 3 ★

if a runner is on 1B, **then** the play is at 3B, and the SS is a
CUTOFF for 3B.

WHY? When the ball is hit to the outfield, the RUNNER on base will
automatically go to 2nd base. So the GENERAL RULE for the
OUTFIELD: your play is *2 bases AHEAD of the RUNNER...*

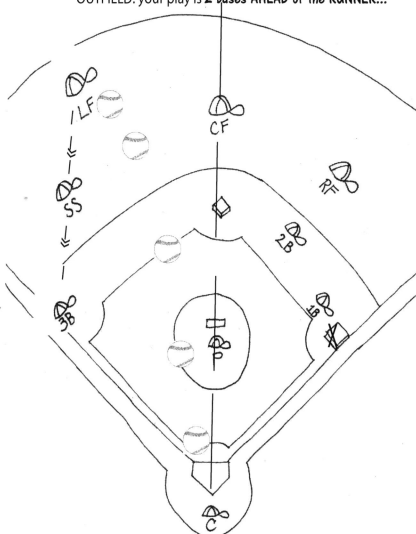

Where to make the play

WHat to do WHeN...

Pretend there is an imaginary line running through the middle of the field.

If the ball is hit to RIGHT FIELD, the 2nd Baseman becomes a CUTOFF for the SS who covers 2nd Base....LF BACKS UP the throw from RF...

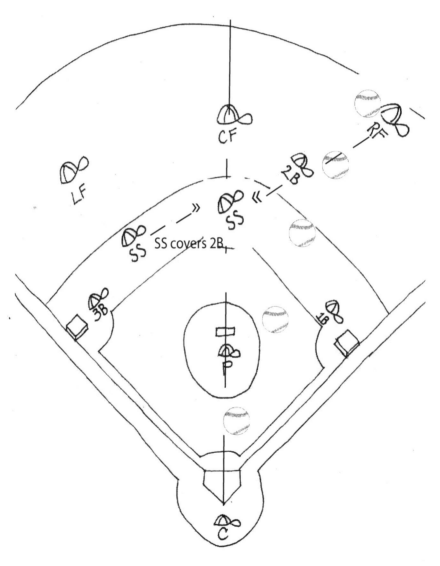

a Ball is Hit to tHe OutFieLd

OR if a runner is on 1B, then the play is at 3B. **then** the play is at 3B. 2B is a CUTOFF for 3B.

WHY? When the ball is hit to the outfield, the RUNNER on base will automatically go to 2nd base. So the GENERAL RULE for the OUTFIELD: your play is 2 bases AHEAD of the RUNNER...

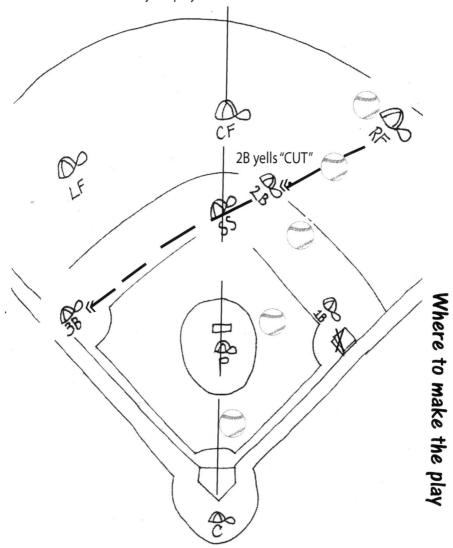

CF

RF

2B yells "CUT"

LF

2B

SS

3B

1B

P

C

Where to make the play

★CUT 4, CUT 4★

MIGHT NEED A 'DOUBLE-CUT'

if a runner is on 2B, then the play is at HOME for the OUTFIELD.
1B goes to the PITCHER's MOUND area,
and the P BACKS UP the C behind HOME PLATE,.
Either the SS or the 2B (depending whether the hit was LF or RF)
is the PRIMARY CUTOFF for OF.

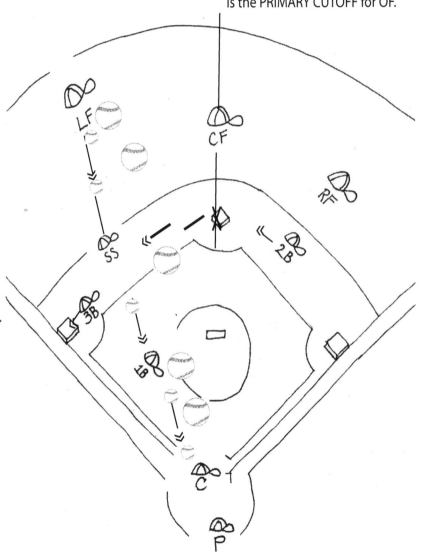

COACH'S NOTES:

AS THE CUTOFF MAN– You need to do the BEST
YOU CAN to be MIDWAY between the THROWER and the
TARGET. You HOLD YOU HANDS UP like FIELD GOALS
yelling "CUT 3, CUT 3, CUT 3" (if play is going to 3).
**You can cheat glove-side with your body to make your transition
quicker.***

AS THE TARGET FIELDER-
You need to LINE UP the CUTOFF MAN by yelling
"LEFT, LEFT, LEFT" or "RIGHT, RIGHT, RIGHT"
to make a STRAIGHT LINE between the THROWER and YOU.

DRILLS FOR SKILLS:

Have an OUTFIELDER, a CUTOFF man and a TARGET--
(either 2B, 3B or HOME, aka '4')

Hit the BALL either in the GAP or LONG FLY BALL.

PRACTICE Players practice LINING UP in a STRAIGHT LINE
with the TARGET.
ALSO CUTOFF MAN practices yelling 'CUT 2, CUT 2,'
and getting body MIDWAY between THROWER
and TARGET....

SITUATIONS....

LOOK tHE Runner Back!

If a RUNNER is on **2nd Base** and NOBODY is on **1st**

OR

A RUNNER is on EVERY BASE *except* 1st

AND the BALL IS HIT TO YOU

THEN

FREEZE the RUNNER by FIELDING THE BALL

Take a moment to **LOOK** at the RUNNER

THEN MAKE THE PLAY AT 1st BASE.

(If they are smart, they should return to the base. But if they run to the next base, or to HOME PLATE, **THROW tHEM OUT!**)

GENERAL RULE-OF-THUMB

If a RUNNER is on base and the ball is hit to the OUTFIELDER, the PLAY is going to be 2 bases in front of them....

RUNNER on 1st, Ball hit to RF, the PLAY will be at 3rd Base...

Where is the Play IF...

there is a RUNNER at 2nd Base? _____

Nobody on Base? _____

TAKE SOME NOTES!

If YOU are the OUTFIELDER and the ball is hit PAST you,
WHAT IS THE PLAYER CALLED
THAT YOU WILL THROW TO?

_____

If YOU are the 2nd Baseman and the ball is hit to the pitcher,
but he misses the ball and you got it.
WHAT DID YOU JUST DO FOR THE
PITCHER?

_____

WHAT IS IT CALLED IF YOU BOTH
MISS IT WHEN IT COULD HAVE
BEEN PLAYED?

_____

If YOU are the 3rd Baseman and the ball is hit just outside
the pitcher's reach, but you can get it.
WHAT IS COVERAGE CALLED?

_____

GOOD JOB! INNING OVER!

MAKE THE PLAY

Crossword Puzzle

Fill in the crossword puzzles with the words that match the clues.

WORDS:

Backing Up	Calling	Error	Freezing
Range	Cutoff	Double Play	

CLUES:

Across
3. A goofed up play
6. Yelling "I GOT IT!"
7. Looking the runner back and holding them at the base

Down
1. When 2 outs are recorded on the same play
2. The act of being behind a player who attempted to get the ball, but the ball passed through to them.
4. Territory covered by a player
5. A supporting player between a deep ball and a target

Did you Learn anything New in this Lesson? List anything you Learned: _____
_____
_____
_____

When you Signed up to play For the team, did you ever play beFore? Describe the team that you played on. Who was on the team? Did you do Well? Describe your Favorite Memory.

L eSSoN 3

HUSTLE BEtWEEn tHE LINES!

Show the coach you want to play by hustling on and off the field. It shows character and and desire to play hard.

It also:
1) Gets your blood pumping
2) Shows enthusiasm and spunk
3) Prepares your mind and body to play hard.

The Objectives for this Lesson are to learn:

Stretching : Conditioning
Nutrition : Fitness
Baseball Muscle Groups

Do you HUSTLE 100% OF tHe tiMe?

In Baseball, running fast and being quick afoot
shows GOOD CHARACTER...

and has a few DISTINCT ADVANTAGES:

1) Prepares your BODY and MIND to
MAKE THE PLAY

2) Gets blood PUMPING!

3) Tells the COACH know YOUR HEART and MIND
are in the game!

BEFORE

you go out and play, FIRST you need to

STRETCH and WARM UP

BATTER UP!

Read the chapter and come back to answer
these questions:

1. Who do you like to WARM UP with?
_____
_____

2. What stretch is your favorite? _____
_____

3. What could happen if you don't stretch?: _____
_____

4. What your ROTATOR CUFF do? _____
_____

5. What is your FAVORITE SNACK before playing baseball? _____
_____

MAJOR MUSCLES USED IN BASEBALL

ROTATOR CUFF (SHOULDER) TRICEPS   BICEPS   PECTORAL (CHEST)
ABS (CORE)   HAMSTRINGS   QUADRICEPS

ROTATOR CUFF: A group of small muscles around the shoulder that allows for the throwing motion.

TRICEPS: Muscles located in the back of your upper arm.

BICEPS: Muscles located in the front of your upper arm.

PECTORAL MUSCLES: The muscles of your chest. These are bigger muscles that allow you to huck the ball with force...among other things...

ABDOMINAL (CORE) MUSCLES: These are muscles around your stomach that provide POWER to your ROTATION when you BAT and THROW.

HAMSTRINGS: The muscle group in the back of the upper portion of your legs.

QUADRICEPS: The muscle group in the front of the upper portion of your legs.

HUSTLE BETWEEN THE LINES

THe PURPOSE OF STRETCHING IS...

STRETCHING

Here are some STRETCHES that focus on BASEBALL MUSCLES!

BEND OVER, TOUCH YOUR TOES!
With straight legs, bend over and touch your toes. Hold for a count of 10. Stretches your HAMSTRING muscles...

CHERRY PICKERS!
Widen your legs and touch the grass and move Left toe-Middle-Right Toe. Stretches HamStrings and Groin.

LUNGES With one leg in front of the other, lean into the stretch. Keep back leg straight and back heel on the ground. Stretches the CALF muscle.

FLaMINGOES!
While one leg is straight and firmly on the ground, bend the other one back until your heel hits your bottom. Grab with your hand and hold for a count of 10 before switching. This stretches your quadriceps.

TRICEPS
With your arm straight up in the air, bend it back, grabbing the elbow with opposite hand to help the stretch. Hold for 10 seconds and switch arms.

BICEPS anD FROnt SHOULDER
Lace hands together behind your back. Slowly raise and extend to feel the stretch.

Back OF SHOULDER
Pull your throwing arm straight across the midline of your chest. Hold for 10 seconds

ROTATOR CUFF Arm CIRCLES! Stick arms straight out at sides and rotate in small circles for count of 10. Then go opposite direction!

TWIStS
While your legs are firmly planted on the ground, rotate at the waist and let your arms swing freely.

...to PREVENT injury!

(strains sprains aches pulls n pains)

CONDITIONING

AS

Run a Lap
A
TEAM

KEREOKES 'BRAIDING'

Line up on a base line and quickly move by crossing over your feet forward and backward, twisting and loosening the hips. Go to 2nd base and back.

QUICK FEET

Line up on a baseline and without crossing your feet, shuffle quickly to 2nd base and back. Keep your body low in 'Ready Position.'

WIND SPRINT 1

Line up on 3rd base line and run with HIGH KNEES to 2nd base.

WIND SPRINT 2

Line up on 3rd baseline and SPRINT to 2nd base.

MORE strength
and FITNESS...

On days you don't practice as a team you can train on your own! Here are some simple exercises you can do at home or in the backyard, or wherever!

HUSTLE BETWEEN THE LINES

RESISTENCE ROPES-Medium tension

Tie one end up about shoulder height through a chain link fence and mimic the throwing motion toward the outfield or away from the fence. Tones tendons and warms up the muscle. Helps prevent injuries.

PUSH UPS

ow many can you do? Test yourself! rst do 10. Then go for more! Try to do at least 20 in a day. Then 30. Keep going!

SIT UPS

Sit Ups help your core muscle group. and develops core muscle strength. Your core strength supports your back and balance. Core muscle strenth will also help you fire the ball in a FROZEN ROPE!

JUMP ROPE

Cardio, cardio, CARDIO! Your heart and lungs need to operate efficiently so YOU DON'T RUN OUT OF ENERGY! They make up your CARDIOVASCULAR system and jumping rope improves your ability to REACT QUICKLY to the ball. And your CALF MUSCLES...

PULL UPS

Find a bar to hang from and lift your chin over the bar...Use your back muscles and biceps. Go for 10!

NOTES ON NUTRITION

YOU REALLY ARE WHAT YOU EAT!!!

HUSTLING, PAYING ATTENTION, REACTING QUICKLY TO THE BALL...

...all require energy. Energy to FOCUS and to be QUICK. Junk food like candy and soda might be tasty, but you can't play for long before you CRASH!

Sustained energy comes from eating food and snacks that are high in protein, vitamins and carbohydrates.

Eat these instead:
Protein Bars
PB & Js
Fruit * Veggies, apples or sugar snap peas
Water / Fruit juices
granola bars

APPLES NUTS WATER

GRANOLA BARS.

Candy, junk food, sugary drinks -- DELICIOUS THEY MAY BE -- are best left to small doses.

PROTEIN BARS

HUSTLE BETWEEN THE LINES

HUSTLING will make your game BETTER!

and shows CHARACTER & LEADERSHIP!

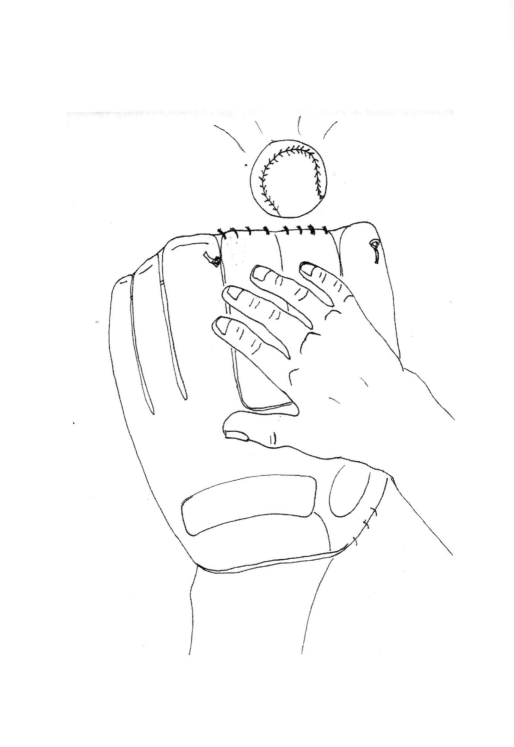

Lesson 4

Catch the Ball with Two Hands

If you have time,
hustle under the ball and set your feet.
Catch the ball
above your head
and throw the ball to the infield
as quick as possible
you just might get the runner out at the base!

The Objectives for this Lesson are to learn:

Ready Position : Catching Strategies
Activities to Practice

GET UNDER THE BALL!

"Get the hang of running under a ball,
setting your feet and
raising BOTH HANDS to catch it over your head.
This is called an **OVERHEAD CATCH.**
Let the ball pound right in the web of your glove.
Once it does, your THROWING hand
should trap the ball
into the ball in the glove,
prohibiting the ball from
bouncing out.
   BEGIN WITH a TENNIS BALL so you don't
hurt yourself if you accidentally miss it...

Two reasons to use 2 hands
when you catch the ball:
1: Prevent the ball from popping out of the glove
(which means LESS ERRORS!)
and
2: Your throwing hand is right there to dig the ball
from your glove and QUICKLY make the throw
to the infield..

REMEMBER::
   YOU CAN'T LET THE BALL GET BEHIND YOU
   AND YOU CAN'T LET IT SAIL OVER YOUR HEAD!

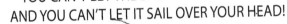

Common BASEBALL TERMS

READY POSITION   2 STEPS BACK   OVERHEAD CATCH

BASKET CATCH   SHOESTRING CATCH

BE ALERT: If the ball looks like it will drop, you have to JUDGE it and choose whether to keep running toward it to catch it, or to let it bounce in front of you.

> If you catch the ball, YOU'RE THE HERO.
> If you miss it, the runner will get EXTRA BASES.
> SOMETIMES ...
> it's better to just give them the SINGLE!
> BUT YOU MUST MAKE AN EFFORT
> TO GET UNDER THE BALL AND CATCH IT

★ BASEBALL TERMS ★ DEFINED

READY POSITION: Legs shoulder width apart, knees bent, glove in front of your body, weight on balls of your feet, and you should be ready to pounce on the ball at the sound of the bat!

2 STEPS BACK: At the sound of the bat, take 2 steps back. This is your 1st move. 2 steps!!! This prevents the ball from getting over your head if the play is close.

GET TO THE SPOT THE BALL WILL DROP BEFORE THE BALL GETS THERE!

OVERHEAD CATCH: When you get to the spot where the ball is dropping, make the catch over your head with 2 hands. (see illustration at front of chapter).

BASKET CATCH: When you catch a ball at or below your waist, you will turn your glove so that it seems like you are catching the ball in a basket, with the glove 'open' towards the sky.

SHOESTRING CATCH: This is a catch made at or below your knees. Generally, you will be 'charging' for the ball and making the catch on the run.

ABCS OF CATCHING A BALL

A: Start in **'READY POSITION'**

B: **2 STEPS BACK** At the sound of the bat, take 2 steps back. Judge the ball: should you 'charge it' or is it going to fly over your head? (some factors to consider are wind and angle of the ball).
A **LINED-DRIVE** is a low-flying, fast hit.
A **POP UP** is a high-flying ball that you can run under for an overhead catch.

C: **CALL IT** Run underneath the ball, calling for it. "I GOT IT!"

D: **TRAP THE BALL** Use glove to catch the ball. Use your non-gloved throwing hand on the back of your glove to trap the ball in the web so it won't pop out.

E: **MAKE A THROW** Dig the ball out with your throwing hand and throw it into the infield.

Batter UP! Test YOUR Skills! MAKE THE CATCH!

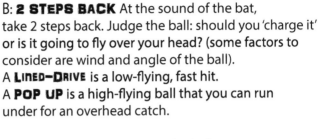

1. When the ball is hit in the air, what is your 1st move?
_____
_____
_____

2. What is READY POSITION?
_____
_____
_____

3. When do you use an OVERHEAD CATCH? _____
_____
_____
_____

4. Describe a BASKET CATCH:
_____
_____
_____

5. What's the difference between a POP UP and a LINED-DRIVE?
_____
_____

PRACTICE ACTIVITIES:

TEE TIME:

1. Play catch with a Tennis Ball: Throw the ball up and run underneath it. Call for it. Use your glove and catch with 2 hands.

ADVANCE YOUR SKILL: Have someone else throw or hit you pop flies and lined-drives with the tennis ball. Work on spotting the ball off the bat and judging flight of path and distance it will travel.

NEXT LEVEL:

2. Play catch with a HARD BALL: This is the same idea as with a tennis ball, but only when you succeed most or all of the time.

ADVANCED YOUR SKILLS:

2. Catch LIVE FLY BALLS, POP UPS, and LINED-DRIVES: Practice judging the ball over long distances. Have someone hit you hard balls from HOME PLATE while you are in the OUTFIELD. Hits should vary in range, from short POP UPS where you have to run in to catch it, or hard hit FLY BALLS that fly overhead.

Practice running backwards while keeping your eye on the ball

VISUALIZE SUCCESS

COLOR IN THE GLOVE AND HAND ON THE PREVIOUS PAGE. WHILE YOU ARE COLORING, THINK OF ALL THE STEPS IN THE ABC Formula.

IN YOUR MIND'S EYE, CAN YOU:

HEAR the CRACK of the bat?

SEE the ball in the air?

FEEL yourself RUNNING UNDER THE BALL and CATCHING it with 2 hands?

Color in the Fielder and List the ABCs of Fielding:

A: _____

B: _____

C: _____

D: _____

E: _____

Lesson 5
Stay Down on the Ball

Stay Low
Get your glove dirty.
Don't let anything go between your legs.
At least hit the ball with your glove to stop it.
Save it from getting past you.
Be courageous!

The Objectives for this Lesson are to learn:

FIELDING GROUND BALLS : FIELDING STRATEGIES :
KEY TERMS : BIG IDEAS

FiELd tHE BaLL iN tHE Mid-LiNE OF your Body

Playing in the infield requires:
1) Knowing how to field a ground ball, and
2) Throwing the ball accurately.

'Staying Down on the Ball' is really important to stop the ball. Use your glove or your body. Guess which one doesn't hurt? Right.

USE YOUR GLOVE!

But be willing and prepared to use your body!

Keep in mind: you still need to use 2 hands, but kind of differently than when you are catching a ball. You'll need to get your glove in the dirt and stay low.

BE TOUGH, BE STRONG. DON'T LET THE BALL GET BY YOU,

Follow the ABCs...

Common BASEBALL TERMS

CHOPPER   SKIMMER   SHORT HOP   BAD HOP

CHARGING THE BALL   SCOOPING VS TRAPPING THE BALL

BattER UP! Test YOUR Skills! MAKE THE PLAY!

1. What does it mean to 'Charge the ball?' _____
_____

2. Describe a 'CHOPPER': _____
_____

3. What does it mean to 'SHORT HOP' the ball? _____
_____

4. Do you like GETTING DIRTY? _____
_____

5. What's the difference between a CHOPPER and a SKIMMER?
_____
_____

BASEBALL TERMS DEFINED

CHOPPER: When a ground ball is hit in high bouncing motion, we call it a "CHOPPER"

SKIMMER: When a ground ball is zipping along the ground and rarely bounces 2 inches off the ground, we call it a 'SKIMMER'

SHORT HOP: When a chopper is coming at you, it's best to 'time it' to scoop it up RIGHT AFTER it takes a bounce. This is 'SHORT HOPPING' the ball. The action happens BELOW your knees.

BAD HOP: When the ball takes an unexpected bounce that makes it unplayable. Bad hops usually occur while you wait for the ball to come to you. That's why 'Charging the Ball' is a good idea!!!

Be Tough But Be Careful: You may need to shield your face with your hand.

DON'T LET THE BALL EAT YOU UP! STAY DOWN ON IT, GET YOUR GLOVE DIRTY, AND SCOOP IT UP! YOU MIGHT EVEN HAVE TO CHARGE IT!

CHARGING THE BALL: When a soft grounder is hit towards you, you have to run to it quickly. This is what we call "CHARGING THE BALL"

SCOOPING VS TRAPPING: When you 'scoop' the ball, the open part of your glove faces the ball. (Just like the picture)... This is better than 'trapping' the ball. 'TRAPPING' the ball is when you attempt to stop the ball by smotheringit on the ground.

ATTENTION: Use 2 hands with ground balls, like the picture. ------>
Your glove is in the dirt, your shoulders and feet are square to the ball, your head is down and your eyes are watching the ball into your mitt.

Field the ball in your midline
Your throwing hand (non-gloved hand) will be above your mitt to both ensure ball is in your glove, and protect your face in case of a bad hop!

Fielding a ground ball

ABCS OF FIELDING A BALL:

A: READY POSITION!

B: REACT and JUDGE THE BALL
At the sound of the bat, judge whether the ball is coming fast, slow, as a chopper or a skimmer. Should you 'charge it?' Factors to consider are how solid the crack of the bat sounded, recognize the spin on the ball and height of the bounces to determine your reaction.

C: QUICK FEET & STAY LOW
Move quickly to get in front of the ball. When you get down to field it, 'SET YOUR FEET,' which means having your left foot towards 1st Base, and your bottom should be low and eyes on the ball. Follow the ball all the way into your glove.

D: WATCH BALL into YOUR MITT
Field the ball in your glove. Have your non-gloved hand about at chest level to shield your face and body from bad hops. Once in the glove, trap the ball with your non-gloved hand.

E: MAKE THE PLAY based on situation

Gametime

PRACTICE ACTIVITIES:

TEE TIME:

1. Throw a tennis ball against a wall and field without a glove:
Practice the ABCs. Use two hands! Stay low!

ADVANCE YOUR SKILL: Have someone else throw you all kinds of
ground balls: choppers, skimmers, to the left, to the right.
Practice getting in front, setting your feet, and using two hands!

> READY POSITION. CHARGE THE BALL. Stay low. Look Ball into Glove.
> Use 2 Hands. Pretend to throw to 1st base.

NEXT LEVEL:

2. Start fielding with a HARD BALL and glove: This is the same
idea as with a tennis ball, but start doing this only when you
succeed most of the time. BUILD CONFIDENCE for LIVE
ACTION!

ADVANCED SKILLS:

2. Field LIVE GROUND BALLS, CHOPPERS, and SKIMMERS: Practice
judging the ball from a position in the infield. Have someone hit you hard
balls from HOME PLATE and practice charging it, setting your feet, and
using two hands. Hits should vary speed. SLOW ROLLERS and BUNTS demand that you
charge them. Choppers demand that you short hop.

VISUALIZE SUCCESS

COLOR IN THE FIELDER. WHILE YOU ARE COLORING, LIST
ALL THE STEPS IN THE ABCs...

CLOSE YOUR EYES AND IMAGINE FIELDING...CAN YOU:
HEAR the CRACK of the bat?

SEE the ball bouncing or skimming toward you? Do you need to go left or right?
Are you watching the ball into your glove?

FEEL the ball stop in your mitt? Are you using 2 hands?

Catching & Fielding Word Search

```
N  O  I  T  I  S  O  P  Y  D  A  E  R  G  T
L  V  W  F  C  B  T  S  A  T  R  C  B  N  W
J  L  D  R  A  M  H  A  E  Q  E  P  A  I  O
W  H  A  D  O  O  G  E  Y  S  P  W  S  R  H
G  K  H  B  R  V  F  U  S  L  P  U  K  T  A
K  O  F  T  G  K  E  N  O  Q  O  D  E  S  N
P  Z  H  J  C  N  G  R  T  O  H  W  T  E  D
A  O  V  I  X  P  I  N  H  O  C  J  Z  O  S
P  O  U  J  B  U  V  G  I  E  Y  U  R  H  B
Q  Q  S  K  I  M  M  E  R  L  A  S  K  S  X
T  W  O  S  T  E  P  S  F  A  L  D  E  O  Q
G  N  I  P  O  O  C  S  N  Y  H  A  Y  T  S
A  V  S  D  A  M  K  N  Q  H  B  C  C  M  H
Y  H  M  P  P  F  I  A  I  C  X  H  B  S  V
J  L  R  T  C  A  E  R  T  J  F  I  V  C  R
```

FIND and CIRCLE the following words in the Word Search:

BAD HOP	BASKET	CALLING
CHARGING BALL	CHOPPER	OVERHEAD
QUICK FEET	REACT	READY POSITION
SCOOPING	SHOESTRING	SHORT HOP
SKIMMER	STAY LOW	TWO HANDS
TWO STEPS		

Did you Learn anything new in this Lesson? List anything you Learned: _____
_____
_____
_____

Describe the best catch and throw play you have ever made...
OR write about your baseball fantasy...or what would you do
if you met your favorite baseball player?

Lesson 6

Throw the Ball Accurately

Throw the ball in a 'Frozen Rope',
NOT a rainbow.
The ball may bounce once or twice
before hitting the target,
but it will get there faster!
With strengthening and practice,
you'll soon throw that 'frozen rope'
right to your target--BULL'S EYE!

The Objectives for this Lesson are to learn:

THROWING TO A TARGET : THROWING MECHANICS :
PITCHING : PITCHING MECHANICS :
KEY TERMS : BIG IDEAS

THROW AT THE CHEST

Practice throwing the ball to the chest of your teammate in a 'FROZEN ROPE.'

The strength comes from your legs and core muscles--very little comes directly from your shoulder or arm.

Push with your leg and rotate your shoulders, FIND THE RELEASE POINT, and let the ball fly!

The 'FROZEN ROPE' you throw might have a bounce or two on the way to its target, but it will have enough speed to beat the runner for the out!"

Common BASEBALL TERMS

FROZEN ROPE   RAINBOW   SETTING YOUR FEET   AIM AT THE CHEST

ROTATING SHOULDERS   RELEASE POINT   WHIP THE WRIST

BATTER UP!

Read the chapter and come back to answer these questions:

1. Explain a 'FROZEN ROPE'? _____
_____

2. Describe a 'RAINBOW' as it applies to throwing a baseball: _____
_____

3. What's the difference between a FROZEN ROPE and a RAINBOW?
_____
_____

4. Describe what it means to 'SET YOUR FEET'? _____
_____

5. What does it mean to 'WHIP THE WRIST'? _____
_____

BASEBALL TERMS DEFINED

FROZEN ROPE: A 'FROZEN ROPE' is when the ball travels in a straight line toward the player. Usually has good velocity.

RAINBOW: When a throw goes in a huge arc, we call it a RAINBOW. Rainbows don't have much speed and the runner is usually safe.

SETTING YOUR FEET: When fielding the ball, SET YOUR FEET. This means that you are balanced and poised to make a strong throw.

> THE POWER OF YOUR THROW COMES FROM YOUR LEGS, CORE MUSCLE GROUPS, THEN SHOULDER, PECs, FOREARMS, and WRIST

AIM AT THE CHEST: An accurate throw across distances means you need a target to aim at. AIMING AT THE CHEST makes it easy for your teammate to catch the ball.

> # KEEP YOUR EYES ON THE TARGET!

ROTATING SHOULDERS: As you begin your throw, the power comes through your core, and you will then ROTATE YOUR SHOULDERS before releasing the ball.

RELEASE POINT: After ROTATING YOUR SHOULDERS, you want to release the ball at a point where it will travel where you aim.

WHIP YOUR WRIST: As you RELEASE THE BALL, the last bit of speed and accuracy comes from WHIPPING YOUR WRIST. This creates a lot of spin on the ball. and takes advantage of all the power generated through your legs.

> **Brain bender:** Do you know how POWERFUL your brain is? KEEP YOUR EYES ON THE TARGET all the way through your throw. The ball will go RIGHT TO THAT SPOT--or close to it--if you follow the ABCs, keep practicing and keep getting stronger!

THROWING THE BALL TO A TARGET

ABCS OF THROWING

A: **SET YOUR FEET** you want a solid
base under you (you don't want to throw
'on the run' or off balance. It's not ideal).

B: **POSITION YOUR BODY** so that your gloved-arm
and shoulder face your target.
RIGHT-HANDERS: Your left foot steps to the target (lead
foot), and you push off your right leg.
LEFT-HANDERS: the opposite. Step with your right foot
(lead foot) and push off with your left.

C: **STEP WITH YOUR LEAD FOOT & PUSH**
While keeping your eye on the target, step to your
target and push from your powerful back foot.

D: **POINT** at your target, and reach back with your
throwing hand.

E: **ROTATE** your hips, body and shoulders
as you sweep your throwing arm across your chest.

F: **RELEASE** THE BALL, and **WHIP** YOUR WRIST.
Use Power! Throw in a straight line in a 'FROZEN ROPE'!
ALWAYS KEEP YOUR EYES ON YOUR TARGET!

1. Keep your arm about a 90 degree angle as it comes forward.
This is what we call 3/4 pitch. Come straight across your chest
with full rotation of your shoulders.

2. Push off your back foot with power!
   Expand and lead with your chest.
      Find the RELEASE POINT!
         Follow through completely with your arm.

ACTIVITIES For PRACTICE

WARM UP!

Grab a buddy and PLAY CATCH.
Practice throwing a ball 10-15 feet apart
for about 10 throws each, then back up 10 feet.
Repeat! 10 throws, 10 feet back. Go to
about 70-80 feet apart.
Come back by 20 feet every 5 throws.
PRaCtICE tHROWING tO tHE CHESt.

Work on MASTERING your throws.
STEP, THROW, STEP THROW...
Right to the target.
FIND YOUR RELEaSE POInt!
Your FROZEN ROPE
will hit the bull's eye in no time!

LONG TOSS:

Throw across long distances of 80-100 feet.
Focus on hitting their chest. Follow the ABCs.
If your FROZEN ROPE falls a couple feet short
and skips in IT's STILL BETTER than a rainbow!

MORE GOOD PRACTICE...

Hit LIVE GROUNDERS and THROW to 1st BASE from 3B, SS and 2B.
Practice SWEEPING your foot across 2nd base as you make a DP!
Hit a 5 gallon bucket that is on top of HOME PLATE
from CENTERFIELD. Pretend it's a runner coming in to score!

VISUALIZE SUCCESS STUDY THE FIELDER MAKING A THROW.
Look at his arm angle. Look at him pushing with his back foot.
ThInK OF tHE StEP—BY—StEP FORMULa!

IN YOUR MIND'S EYE, CAN YOU:

HEAR the ball snap in your glove, your cleats dig in the dirt as you throw
to your target?

SEE the ball release from your hand. You watch it go right into
the 1st baseman's glove?

FEEL the ball release. Feel the adrenylin rush of beating the
runner to make the out? GooD JOB!

THROWING ACCURATELY

PITCHERS: Take Command
of the Game

Pitching requires the skill to throw accurately. Study, apply, practice and execute the ABCs of throwing. The next level is becoming a reliable and confident pitcher.

As a pitcher, your approach is to put the ball INTO YOUR CATCHER'S GLOVE. DON'T TAKE YOUR EYES OFF THAT GLOVE! Take command of the game by having command of your pitch. I tell my pitchers to "pitch for contact." That way, the batter puts the ball into play, gets the defense involved, gets 3 quick out and saves their arm.

► RELAX & HAVE FUN! ◄

Once you know the ABCs by heart, you can do the most important thing: FORGET ABOUT 'EM! OVERTHINKING kills pitching. When you overthink, you need to BREATHE, repeat the ABCs, then clear your mind and ROCK 'N FIRE. Just throw the ball and hit the glove!

Common BASEBALL TERMS

WINDUP   THE STRETCH   THE RUBBER   STRIKE ZONE

FAST BALL   OFF-SPEED PITCH   WILD PITCH   A BALK

1. Describe the 'STRIKE ZONE'? _____

_____

2. Describe a 'WINDUP': _____

_____

3. What's the difference between the 'WINDUP' and the 'STRETCH'?

_____

_____

4. What's the difference between a FAST BALL and a CHANGE UP'?

_____

_____

5. What does it mean to throw an 'OFF SPEED PITCH'? _____

_____

BASEBALL TERMS DEFINED

WINDUP: The WINDUP is a sequence of motions used by the pitcher to get the most momentum and power behind their pitch. It consists of: ROCKING BACK, KICKING, and pushing off THE RUBBER. When no runners are on base, or when a runner is on 3rd and is no longer a threat to steal, a pitcher uses THE WINDUP.

THE STRETCH: A pitching motion used when runners are on base and a threat to steal a base. It is faster than the WINDUP. The pitcher's foot is SET in THE RUBBER from the start (unlike the WINDUP) and the pitcher KICKS and pushes without rocking back to get extra momentum. It's quicker, but harnesses less power from momentum than the WINDUP.

THE RUBBER: The white block that pitchers push off for power.

A BALK: An infraction caused by the pitcher. Many rules apply here, but generally, it's a failed attempt to set yourself and cleanly deliver the ball to the catcher. If a runner is on base, they are rewarded with moving up a base.

> **EYES Always ON THE CATCHER's GLOVE!**

STRIKE ZONE: The IMAGINARY zone above home plate that consists of the width of home plate, and starts at the batter's knees and goes up to the letters on the batter's jersey.

FAST BALL: The fastest pitch in a pitcher's arsenal of pitches. There is a 4-seam, 2-seam and split-finger fast ball. The difference is in how the pitcher holds the ball in relation to the seams.

OFF SPEED PITCH: A pitch that looks like a fast ball, but comes inslower and oftentimes has movement. This can be a 'CHANGE UP,' a 'KNUCKLE BALL,' or a 'SLIDER.'

WILD PITCH: A pitch that goes anywhere but it's intended spot. Usually a wild pitch is one that is in the dirt and passes the catcher.

ABCS OF PITCHING:

BREATHE & RELAX
Take a deep breath, relax your shoulders. Recite the ABCs to yourself. Then, just think about having fun.

A: **ROCK & KICK** Place your foot in the rubber, find your target. Rock back, strengthen your back leg. KICK YOUR LEG UP (closest one to catcher-- the one you'll step with) and

B: **PUSH HARD** off the rubber with your power leg. Extend your front leg towards the catcher. Land your foot 'pointing' towards the catcher.

C: **EXPAND & LEAD** with your chest. Keep your eyes on the catcher's glove. Point your gloved-hand toward the catcher's glove. Reach back with your throwing hand.

D: **ROTATE** your shoulders as you bring your arm around

E: **RELEASE POINT** Find the 'RELEASE POINT' that consistently finds the target on a FROZEN ROPE.

F: **FOLLOW THROUGH** and bend your back.

G: **EYES ON CATCHER'S GLOVE!**
Keep your eyes on the catcher's glove AT ALL TIMES!

REPEAT! Muscle memory will kick in after about 50 pitches...APPLY & EXECUTE during practice.

TRAINING TIP: You can place a baseball in a sock and practice the ABCs. Hold the end of the sock and rock 'n fire.
DON'T LET GO OF SOCK AS YOU PRACTICE THE THROWING MOTION.
This helps prevent injury when you actually pitch.

ACTIVITIES FOR PRACTICE:

LONG TOSS FOR PITCHING

APPLY the ABCs in Long Toss of about 60 feet. It improves the PUSH OFF and knowing one's RELEASE POINT. Use a 'CROW HOP' to generate force. Throw a 'FROZEN ROPE.' Throw only about 20 pitches at this distance. Stretches out muscles and increases strength.

PITCHING & CATCHING:

Apply the ABCs on a pitcher's mound with a catcher. KEEP YOUR EYES ON THE CATCHER'S GLOVE! Start at 70% effort to establish your release point and your mental zone. Work up to 90%, then 100% strength.

THE ART OF ILLUSION

As a Pitcher, Your Object is to make a batter swing at balls and watch strikes go by. The old saying goes: "Get 'em In with Strikes, Get 'em Out with balls!

LIST THE ABCs OF PITCHING:

A: _____
B: _____
C: _____
D: _____
E: _____
F: _____
G: _____
H: _____

VISUALIZE SUCCESS

LOOK AT THE PITCHER MAKING A THROW. WHILE YOU ARE LOOKING, THINK OF ALL THE STEPS IN THE ABCs.

IN YOUR MIND'S EYE, YOU:

HEAR nothing. YOU ONLY FOCUS ON YOUR VISION OF THE GLOVE!

SEE the way you rock, kick, expand your chest, step, rotate, release, follow through and see the ball right into the catcher's glove.

FEEL the release of the ball. Feel your back foot push off the rubber. Feel your body's momentum square up to the batter. Feel the rush of throwing STRIKE 3!

THrOWiNg AccUrateLy CrossWord

Across
6. By doing this, you create spin, speed and accuracy in your throw
7. a pitch that comes in slower than a fastball
11. Fastest pitch in the pitcher's arsenal
12. The white block pitchers push off for power
Down
1. When the ball travels in a straight line to the target
2. the zone above home plate between the batter's knees and jersey letters
3. When the ball travels in a HUGE arc
4. When nobody is on base, this is the type of pitching sequence the pitcher uses
5. When runners are on base, the pitcher uses this pitching sequence
6. a pitch that is in the dirt and passes the catcher
8. Your shoulders do this during the throw
9. the moment when you let go of the ball
10. A failed attempt by the pitcher to set themselves

Did you learn anything new in this lesson? List anything you learned: _____

_____

_____

_____

Do you want to pitch? If so, what's your favorite pitch?
Describe how you hold the ball. Describe the best
experience you've had as a pitcher.
If you don't pitch, tell about the best time you were part of
a play that resulted in an out.

_____

_____

_____

_____

_____

_____

_____

_____

_____

_____

_____

_____

_____

_____

_____

_____

_____

_____

_____

_____

_____

_____

_____

Do you REALLY want to hit the ball?

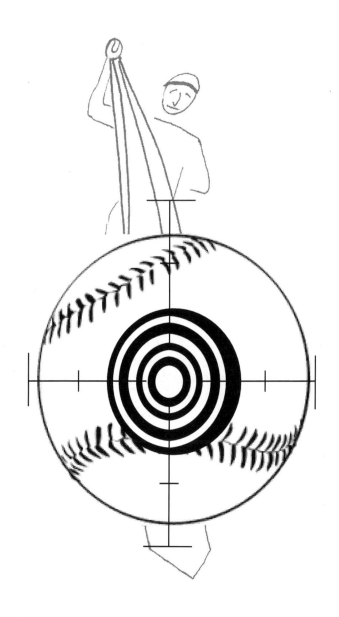

COLOR IN THE ILLUSTRATION AND IMAGINE CRUSHING THE MIDDLE OF THE BALL, RIGHT IN THE MIDDLE OF THE TARGET...

LeSSoN 7
CuT tHE BaLL in HALF

Master the art of hitting line drives.
Focus on seeing the middle of the ball
Cut it in half

Don't overswing--you'll pull your head

It's a better habit to hit for in the gaps
for a SINGLE or DOUBLE than trying to
hit a HOME RUN.

The Objectives for this Lesson are to learn:

The RITUAL of BATTING : HITTING TACTICS :
KEY TERMS : MAXIMIZING FORCE

HAVE A QUICK BAT...

The most exciting part about playing baseball is **Batting**! (Besides diving for a ball, or making a double play...). For a few minutes, you get your chance to hit the ball, run the bases and score some runs!

When you go up to bat, make a **RItUaL** out of it. Do the same thing each time as your prepare for a pitch. Take a **DEEP BREatH**, repeat the ABCs, line up your knuckles and **DIG In** the batter's box with your back foot. Take a practice swing and show the pitcher your **WHEELHOUSE**. Then get in your stance and be ready.

KNOW YOUR SWING
KNOW THE STRIKE ZONE

The key to success is **tIMING.** Focus on the ball from the pitcher's hand to the plate. Find the middle of the ball and **CUt It In HaLF**. It's very important that you swing quickly! Yep, hit the ball right in the middle. Give it a solid Ka-POW!!! Know your swingand PRACTICE PRACTICE PRACTICE!

Batter UP!
Read the chapter and come back to answer these questions:

1. Where do you like 'YOUR PITCH'?
ex: low and inside, or at my belly...
_____
_____
_____

2. Where is your 'WHEELHOUSE'?:
_____
_____
_____

3. What does it mean to 'STEP INTO THE PITCH'?
_____
_____

4. What's the difference between a HALF SWING and a 'FULL SWING'?
_____
_____
_____

5. When do you 'CHOKE UP' on the bat? Why?_____
_____
_____

...& HIT LINE DRIVES

Common BASEBALL TERMS

BATTER'S BOX   YOUR PITCH   STEP INTO THE PITCH   LEVEL SWING

WHEELHOUSE   FULL SWING   LINE DRIVE   CHOKE UP   BUNT

★ BASEBALL TERMS ★ DEFINED

YOUR PITCH: This is all about YOU-the batter. Do you like the pitch at your waist? At the knees? Or at the chest? Where does your swing naturally cut through the strike zone? Wherever your 'sweet spot' is, that is 'YOUR PITCH.' Your job is to find 'YOUR PITCH' from the pitcher's hand.

STEP INTO THE PITCH: To get a good, solid hit with force and power, you need to step toward the pitcher as the ball is coming to you. HAVE COURAGE! Don't back out of the box for fear of getting hit. Step into the pitch and swing the bat and hit the ball!

LEVEL SWING: When you have your back elbow up, and you lead the bat through the strike zone with your front arm, it should produce a LEVEL SWING through the strike zone. No chops, and no upper cuts. Just a nice LEVEL swing around waist high.

WHEELHOUSE: This is the area in which YOUR PITCH travels. Your WHEELHOUSE is every pitch you can handle--whether slightly high, low, inside or outside. If you can get some solid crack of the bat on the ball, this is your pitch. DON'T GET FOOLED BY PITCHES OUTSIDE YOUR WHEELHOUSE!

FULL SWING: Many new players hit the ball and stop their swing half way. A FULL SWING is one where you 'follow through' with full rotation of the hips, shoulders and arms. This follow through keeps the full power of the swing and provides important momentum to drive the ball.

CHOKE UP: When you have 2 strikes on you, move your hands up about a half inch. This increases bat speed to get a piece of the ball for a potential single.

BUNT: When you 'square around' and simply tap the ball with your bat to place the ball in the area between the pitcher and catcher, down the 3rd baseline or 1st baseline. AKA "SMALL BALL"

ABCS OF BATTING:

A: **'DIG IN'** with your back foot.
Dig out a small hole for your foot. This keeps your back foot in place. You want to use this foot for power.

B: **BODY POSITION:** Your body faces home plate--not the pitcher! Both of your toes point toward home plate.

C: **KNEES BENT,**
SHOULDERS RELAXED,
KNUCKLES LINED UP,
BACK ELBOW UP,
STAY RELAXED...

D: **LEVEL SWING**: As you get into your stance, remember: Keep your back elbow level with your shoulder! Keep your bat off your shoulder.

E: **PRACTICE CUT:** Before the pitch, softly swing the bat through the zone where you want the ball thrown. This is called your **'WHEELHOUSE.'** This is where, when the ball is pitched, you'll crush it with the **'SWEEt SPOt'** of the bat.

F: **SEE tHE BALL** as it leaves the hand of the pitcher. Follow the ball and find **tHE CENTER** of it.

G: **TIME YOUR SWING:** As the pitch leaves the pitcher's hand, start your swing by:

1. **STEPPING TO THE PITCH,**
ROTATE YOUR HIPS,
FLEX YOUR GUT

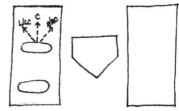

2. **MOVE** your hands to the ball.
3. **CUT THE BALL IN HALF**
4. **MAKE A FULL SWING** to continue the POWER.

★ **MAKE A RITUAL** ★
COMING TO BAT

DRILLS For SKILLS:

TEE WORK: KNOW YOUR SWING

Practice your LEVEL swing and ALL STEPS of the ABCs.
Concentrate on the middle of the ball.
VISUALIZE HITTING FOR A SINGLE...Nice and Easy...

SOFT TOSS: Great for incorporating all steps of the swing into one motion. Have someone lightly toss you a ball as you hit it into a net or fence. Concentrate on finding the middle of the ball.
VISUALIZE BEFORE YOU HIT!: Practice hitting to an imaginary Left Field, then Center, then Right.

PLAY PEPPER

with teammates, friends or family: Great for hand-eye coordination, building strength in forearms, wrists, hands, and work on TIMING.
HIT THE CENTER OF THE BALL!

How to play: Have 3 friends take turns throwing the ball to a batter from about 8-10 feet away. The batter needs to hit the ball to them on the ground to be 'SAFE.' DO NOT HIT WITH A FULL SWING. Batter should make a solid half swing using a lot of wrist and hand strength.
If a lined-drive is caught, you're OUT! ROTATE!

LIVE PITCH BATTING PRACTICE --

One Pitcher. One Batter. Infielders, outfielders.
Simulate a game situation. Puts all the ABCs together: locating the ball out of pitcher's hand, finding the center of the ball, TIMING of the step into the pitch and a QUICK swing to CUT THE BALL IN HALF! Builds confidence and the KA-POW! that you need to be a strong hitter.

REMEMBER!
EXERCISE DISCIPLINE

RECOGNIZE a BALL from a STRIKE
Don't swing at BALLS out of the STRIKE ZONE!!!

FORCE = MASS X VELOCITY

FORCE is HOW MUCH POWER is TRANSFERRED at IMPACT
from YOUR BAT to THE BALL

MASS is the WEIGHT the BAT. In the equation, Mass = X^2

VELOCITY is the SPEED of the BAT at IMPACT. In the equation,
Velocity = X^4

⟩ BAT SPEED IS MOST IMPORTANT ⟨

WHIP the WEIGHT of your bat THROUGH THE STRIKE ZONE.
GENERATE FORCE that meets the ball which is coming
in an opposite direction with its own VELOCITY.
WATCH THE BALL HIT THE BAT!
THE RESULT is a KA-POW! that BLASTS the ball in a LINE DRIVE
when you 'CUt tHE BaLL In HaLF'...

CoLor in the Scene and...

...VISUALIZE SUCCESS

WHILE YOU ARE COLORING, THINK OF ALL THE STEPS IN THE ABCs.
TAKE A MOMENT--CLOSE YOUR EYES AND:

SEE the bat SLICING THROUGH the ball, just in front of home plate. Do you see yourself crush a line drive over the Shortstop into Left-Center Field?

HEAR the bat CONNECT WITH the ball. :: Ka-POW! ::

FEEL yourself burst out of the BATTER'S BOX and RUNNING to 1st Base?

HIT FOR A SINGLE IN THE GAPS!

Batting & Best Effort Word Search

```
J  A  R  B  N  C  Y  A  G  W  V  F  C  C  U
F  F  U  P  W  S  B  L  H  K  Y  Z  H  Y  J
G  N  X  O  B  S  R  E  T  T  A  B  O  Q  I
T  N  B  G  S  V  E  H  E  T  Y  Z  K  P  N
F  V  I  U  N  L  F  C  B  T  R  P  E  L  O
N  O  Y  W  H  I  I  G  P  O  E  D  U  G  L
C  P  R  O  S  F  M  D  Z  P  P  B  P  F  S
T  T  U  E  I  L  G  I  E  S  P  K  J  T  Y
Q  S  B  R  H  Y  L  U  T  T  E  X  Y  M  B
E  T  C  N  X  A  K  U  Z  E  P  Y  L  L  D
B  A  C  K  H  A  N  D  F  E  P  E  O  N  R
S  F  O  R  C  E  G  D  C  W  A  O  E  V  E
E  V  I  D  A  Z  C  W  L  S  P  T  I  M  A
Q  P  T  Z  Z  A  J  W  Q  E  X  P  I  C  C
L  A  U  T  I  R  V  P  R  E  R  F  H  A  T
```

FIND and CIRCLE the following words in the Word Search:

BACKHAND	BATTERSBOX	BLOOPER
BUNT	CHOKEUP	DIVE
EXTEND	FORCE	FOREHAND
FULLSWING	PEPPER	REACT
RITUAL	SACRIFICE	SLIDE
SWEETSPOT	TIMING	WHEELHOUSE

Did you learn anything new in this lesson? List anything you learned: _____
_____
_____
_____

Describe the best hit you've ever had. Was it deep? Was it a lined-drive? Did it score some runs?...Give some detail. How did it feel?
_____
_____
_____
_____
_____
_____
_____
_____
_____
_____

What was the best effort you made to get a ball? Did you have to dive for it? Did you have to take it off the chest? Describe everything about it with details. What did it sound like or feel like?
_____
_____
_____
_____
_____
_____
_____
_____
_____

DRAW YOURSELF DIVING, SLIDING, HUSTLING, OR CRUSHING THE BALL...

LESSON 8

BEST EFFORT=DIVING, SLIDING, EtC

Constantly demand the best from yourself.
Strive for excellence
Rise above challenges
Shake off errors, strike outs, and blunders...

When your HUNGER for GREATNESS
is BIGGER than your FEAR of fallin' short,
then you will GIVE ALL YOU'VE GOT
and make PHENOMENAL plays happen...

When this is your TRUTH,
There is no limit to your POTENTIAL
and you will witness MAGIC
in YOURSELF.

The Objectives for this Lesson are to learn:

EFFORT = AWESOME : FIGURE 4 SLIDING :
DIVING FOR THE BALL : KEY TERMS : BIG IDEAS

GET HUNGRY For VICTORY!

EFFORT = AWESOME!

You can't CONTROL outcomes.
What you CAN control is YOUR EFFORT!
EFFORT MAKES MAGIC happen!
IF you HUSTLE, and give your BEST EFFORT
GUESS WHAT! You might SURPRISE yourself
with a PHENOMENAL play!
MAGIC comes in many shapes & sizes.
In baseball, you make MAGIC with your GLOVE,
BAT, LEGS, ARM & HEART!
When you are HUNGRY for VICTORY, you HUSTLE!
You EAT THAT BALL UP or
BEAT THAT THROW!
You'll REACT quickly, DIVE and BACKHAND
the ball and MAKE THE PLAY.
GET DIRTY!

Then LISTEN...THE CROWD GOES WILD!....AHHHHH!

More importantly, you'll stop a runner from being on base,
Every runner on base is a potential threat to score...

If you are STRETCHing a
SINGLE into a DOUBLE,
or you are RACING around
3rd going to HOME,
you might need to
SLIDE under the tag.

★ BE CONSERVATIVELY AGGESSIVE ★
ON THE BASES

Don't OVERRUN the base or GET CAUGHT in a PICKLE!
BE a THREAT, but don't be FOOLISH! KEEP YOUR EYES
ON THE BALL...KNOW YOUR SPEED! BE SAFE!

Common **BASEBALL TERMS**

FIGURE 4 SLIDE   HEADFIRST SLIDE   COMMIT TO THE BALL

Batter UP! Tell YOUR story!

1. What's the difference between
          a HEADFIRST slide and a FIGURE 4 slide?

_____

_____

2. Write about a time you COMMITTED TO THE BALL: _____

_____

_____

_____

_____

3. Describe the BEST PLAY you ever made:

_____

_____

_____

_____

EFFORT = PHENOMENAL PLAYS

EFFORT = MAGIC

GOLDEN FORMULA FOR
          a **FIGURE 4 SLIDE:**

A: **RUN**! Hard and fast to the base.

B: **BEGIN** SLIDE about a body length and a 1/2
          away from the base.

C: **CROSS** Right leg under left leg. Left leg
          EXTENDS outward with slight bend
          in the knees to the bag.

D: **STAY** LIGHT through the slide. That means
          don't just !PLUMP! and fall, but be agile.

SL—IIIIIII—DE

E: **STAY DOWN** OR **POP UP!**
          Depending on the situation---
If the DEFENSE was trying to tag you out, stay down.
If you were beating the throw by a mile,
          SPRING UP!
LISTEN TO COACH to know if you should run to the next base...

DRILLS For SKILLS:

HOW FAST YOU RUN will determine where you need to begin your slide. DRILL: Line up on first base. Take off in a full sprint to 2nd base. Execute the FIGURE 4 SLIDE.

RUN FAST AND HARD!

NEXT LEVEL:
Execute the DRILL above, but now try to run so fast and PRETEND the ball gets by the Outfielder & **POP UP** and take off to 3rd!

ADVANCED SKILLS:
WHEN the CATCHER is trying to throw to 2B to get a runner that is stealing, the ball comes to the FRONT CORNER.
PRACTICE: SLIDE AWAY from the ball toward the OUTSIDE CORNER (toward OF) to avoid the tag.

ALSO, when the ball is in LF and is coming toward 2B, it comes toward the Left side of the bag.
PRACTICE sliding toward the RIGHT SIDE of the bag to avoid the tag.

CLOSE YOUR EYES. You are on 1B and the Coach just gave you the steal sign...
IMAGINE as the ball crosses the plate, YOU GET A GREAT JUMP.
You HUSTLE with your HEAD DOWN, DIGGING HARD---

HEAR the WIND in your EARS.

SEE the BASE getting closer

FEEL yourself EXECUTE the FIGURE 4 SLIDE-- SAFE! You BEAT the THROW! GOOD JOB!

VISUALIZE SUCCESS

Effort makes incredible things HAPPEN!

ABCS OF DIVING FOR THE BALL

A: **REACT!** to the sound of the bat.

B: **MOVE YOUR FEET!** Do your best
to get in front of the ball.

C: **EXTEND** outstretch your body and glove to
at least knock ball down but intentionally
to glove it

E: **LOOK** the ball into your glove at ALL TIMES!

F: **SOFTEN** your landing with your bare hand
and knees. Then POP UP, SET YOUR FEET
and throw!

DRILLS For SKILLS

HAVE SOMEONE throw you ground balls from 10 feet away that are just out of reach. Dive for them. Execute the ABCs...

Use **BACKHAND** and **FOREHAND** techniques.

KEEP YOUR EYE ON THE BALL!
LOOK THE BALL INTO YOUR GLOVE!

VISUALIZE SUCCESS

CLOSE YOUR EYES. You are on the diamond at your favorite position. IMAGINE yourself REACTING to a ball hit to your right. It seems far off but not TOO FAR. You can still make a play, but it requires EXTRA EFFORT! DIVE for the ball as you get close to it. LISTEN and

HEAR the CRACK of the bat.

SEE the ball skimming to your left or right
DID YOU REACT QUICKLY ENOUGH?

FEEL the ball hit your mitt. YOU GOT IT!
Now, SPRING TO YOUR FEET and THROW!

AND THE CROWD GOES WILD!!!!!!!!!

EFFORT PROVES HEART

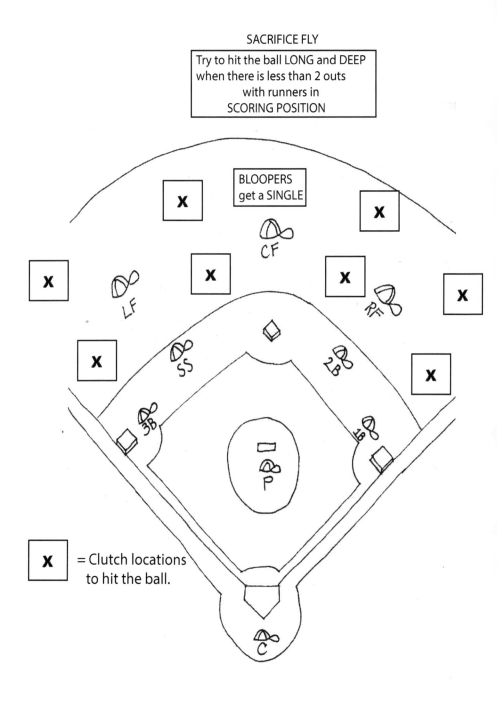

Lesson 9
Be a Clutch Hitter

Runners on 2nd and 3rd, 2 Outs,
Bottom of the inning.
ALL you need is a basehit.

Time for you to master
the Art of 'CLUTCH' hitting...

The Objectives for this Lesson are to learn:

ART OF CLUTCH : SACRIFICE : SQUEEZE PLAYS :
BASEBALL TERMS : BIG IDEAS

WHEN IT ABSOLUTELY MATTERS...

"We've all dreamed about the moment:
Bottom of the 9th, 2 Outs, bases loaded,
tie game...What do YOU think comes next?

The next line that usually comes is:
Here's the pitch...He swings and hits
a TOWERING FLY BALL...The fielder is
going BACK BACK BACK...
a GRAND SLAM!!!.....

That is a GREAT dream.

But all the TEAM really wants is:

A CLUTCH HIT

What is a CLUTCH HIT?

Whenever a runner is on 2nd or 3rd base (aka 'scoring positon')
and you manage to get a hit or get on base, and move
the runner forward, we call it

a 'CLUTCH' HIT.

Let's be clear: EVERY time you come to bat, you have an
OPPORTUNITY to help your team. Whether it's the
1st inning or the LAST inning, you have a chance to
GET ON BASE and be a THREAT to score.

ARE THERE TIMES WHEN YOUR 'UPS' ARE MORE IMPORTANT THAN OTHERS?

ABSOLUTELY! Take the previous scenario: 1 run can WIN the game.
Your time at bat is EXTREMELY important in the LATE innings!

In comparison, you can't 'WIN' the game in the 1st inning,
but you can CONTRIBUTE to building a lead for your team.

Common **BASEBALL TERMS**

CLUTCH HIT   BLOOPER   TIMING   SQUEEZE PLAY

HIT BY PITCH   STAYING ALIVE   SACRIFICE

Being **CLUTCH** means that you

STAY WITHIN YOUR GAME

don't **OVERSWING** by having thoughts of a HOME RUN.

HIT FOR A SINGLE, make a nice EASY SWING...

THINK 'LINE DRIVE,' find the ball out of the pitcher's hand and...

Cut tHE BaLL in HaLF...

Find YOUR PITCH, HAVE DISCIPLINE, BE RELIABLE...

When it's late in the game, and the GAME IS ON THE LINE,
getting on base with a hit, a walk, a bunt, or being
HIT BY THE PITCH (on accident of course)
can BUILD MOMENTUM and get you a VICTORY.

 **THAT MEANS YOU ARE CLUTCH!**

WHAT DO YOU KNOW
ABOUT CLUTCH HITTING:

Read the chapter and come back to answer these questions:

What does the term SACRIFICE FLY mean? Explain how it's 'CLUTCH'?

_____
_____
_____

What's the difference between a blooper and a lined-drive? How can a BLOOPER be 'CLUTCH'?

_____
_____
_____

Bases loaded. Tie game. The count is 1 ball, 2 strikes. The pitch came inside and grazed your shoulder. How is that 'CLUTCH'?

_____
_____
_____

What is a SQUEEZE PLAY? How is a SQUEEZE PLAY fit the term 'CLUTCH'?_____
_____
_____

Bases are loaded. 2 outs, last inning. The count is 3 balls 2 strikes. You swing and hit the ball just foul. Are you out?

_____
_____
_____

It's 3 balls, 2 strikes, 1 out, baserunner on 3rd. Should you 'swing for the fence'? Why or why not?

_____
_____
_____

BASEBALL TERMS DEFINED

CLUTCH HIT
A hit when the game is on the line. A CLUTCH HITTER is one that can be relied on to get on base.

BLOOPER
A BLOOPER is a simple POP FLY just over an infielder into shallow outfield. Usually a single. If a runner is on 3rd base, they can score!

SQUEEZE PLAY/SUICIDE SQUEEZE
When a runner is on 3rd base and the batter is asked to BUNT the ball in order to SCORE the runner, it's called a SQUEEZE PLAY. If the runner is also asked to STEAL HOME when the batter is asked to BUNT, it's called a SUICIDE SQUEEZE PLAY, because there is no turning back.

HIT BY PITCH
When a pitch comes too far inside and hits the batter. The batter is awarded 1st base.

SACRIFICE
INTENTIONALLY hitting into an out to ULTIMATELY benefit your team. Example: When the batter hits a LONG FLY ball to an outfielder surely resulting in an OUT, but a baserunner can TAG UP, the batter hit a SACRIFICE FLY.

TIMING
The perfect synchronicity between the ball hitting the bat or the runner sliding under a tag or beating a throw to be SAFE. Baseball is all about TIMING.

STAYING ALIVE
FOULing the ball with 2 strikes. You are NOT out. You just STAYED ALIVE!

CLUTCH HITTING:

PARTS OF THE FIELD
TO PLACE THE BALL

sacrifice fly

Try to hit the ball LONG and DEEP
when there is less than 2 outs
with runners in
SCORING POSITION

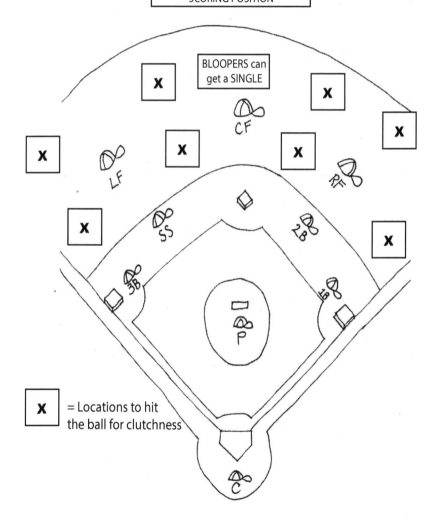

BLOOPERS can get a SINGLE

X = Locations to hit the ball for clutchness

SQUEEZE PLAY/
SUICIDE SQUEEZE

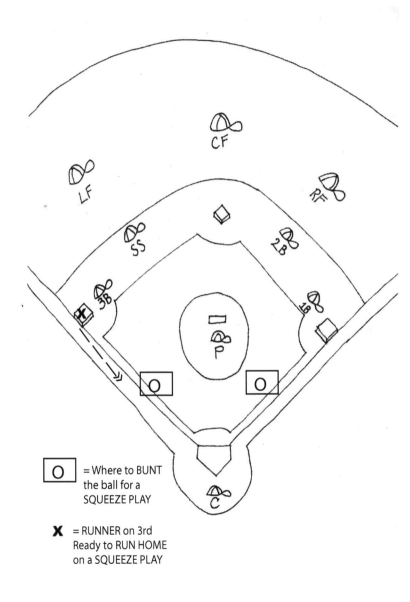

CF

LF

RF

SS

2B

3B

1B

P

O   O

C

| O | = Where to BUNT the ball for a SQUEEZE PLAY |

X = RUNNER on 3rd Ready to RUN HOME on a SQUEEZE PLAY

Lesson 10

Be the Hero

You must BELIEVE
You can RISE to the challenge.
Block out any FEAR by being BRAVE.
You are STRONGER than you think.
You can TAKE what the GAME gives you.

When you BELIEVE in YOURSELF and
Get in front of a sizzling ground ball
to MAKE A PLAY,
Others BELIEVE in you as well.
You BECOME a HERO for your teammates.
You BECOME an INSPIRATION for others
to RISE to the challenge and
abandon their fears as well...

The Objectives for this Lesson are to learn:

> ESSENTIALS of COURAGE : CARDINAL RULE :
> KEY TERMS : BIG IDEAS

Be Mentally Tough...

BE THE HERO

When you act COURAGEOUSLY in baseball,
and BRAVELY go for that ball, chances are,
YOU'LL MAKE THE PLAY!
You HAVE to RISE to the CHALLENGE!

BE COURAGEOUS!

"You understand now that you HAVE to give 100%
of your effort AT ALL TIMES.

GREAT things will happen when you GIVE YOUR ALL!

That is the same throughout LIFE:
with SCHOOL, HOBBIES, and HELPING others --
ESPECIALLY those who LOVE & SUPPORT YOU.

THE CARDINAL RULE :

GIVE EVERYTHING YOU GOT,
and then GIVE A LITTLE MORE!

...You will be richly rewarded...

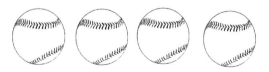

...ANd PHySiCaLLy Strong!

In Baseball, the same rule applies, only slightly differently. When a groundball is SIZZLING toward you, it's natural to have FEARS of that ball.

> COURAGE is about RISING ABOVE fears
> & BRAVELY getting in front of the ball

8 teammates are counting on you.

But, sometimes things don't go the way you planned.

Sometimes the ball takes a BAD HOP!

HOW DO YOU PLAN FOR a BAD HOP?

You need to be PHYSICALLY STRONG and MENTALLY TOUGH!

Use the skills & fundamentals you learned here.
Use your bare hand to shield your face, mouth and nose.
Tighten your muscles.

YOUR MUSCLES ARE YOUR BODY ARMOR!

GET IN FRONT & STOP THE BALL!

Remember: IF you take a ball off the body....

> PAIN IS ONLY AN INSTANT, BUT GLORY IS FOREVER!!!

SHAKE it OFF! You'll be talking about that great play
and many more like it
for DAYS TO COME!!!

Common **BASEBALL TERMS**

COMMITMENT   COURAGE   GLORY

SCOREBOARD

BatteR UP! Test YOUR Skills! Get a GOOD HIT!

1. Describe a moment you
needed to have COURAGE?'

_____
_____
_____
_____
_____
_____

2. Brag about yourself.
List 5 ways you have
BEEN A HERO for your team:

1_____
2_____
3_____
4_____
5_____

3. What does it mean to
COMMIT to the ball?

_____
_____
_____
_____
_____

4. Explain the following
                    statement:
"PAIN IS ONLY AN INSTANT
        BUT GLORY IS FOREVER"?

_____
_____
_____
_____

BASEBALL TERMS DEFINED

COMMITMENT: When you are determined and focused, and move to the ball to make the play. You are WILLING to SACRIFICE your BODY.

COURAGE: The GUTS to GET IN FRONT of the ball, STAY LOW & MAKE THE PLAY.

GLORY: When you HAVE COURAGE and either MAKE THE PLAY, or STOP THE BALL at ALL COSTS to your body Your TEAMMATES will EXPLODE with SUPPORT & APPLAUSE... my friend, THAT's GLORY!

COMMIT TO THE BALL & BE THE HERO!!!

DO IT FOR YOUR:

COACH

TEAMMATES

PARENTS, FANS

& YOURSELF!

MOST OF ALL:
HAVE FUN PLAYING THE GREAT GAME OF BASEBALL!!!

Made in the USA
Las Vegas, NV
15 July 2021